Wake Up to the World of Science

THE WORLD OF INSECTS

B. Bornancin

Burke Books ▶ LONDON ∗ TORONTO ∗ NEW YORK

CONTENTS

Notes

1 When you read x 3 (or another number) beneath a photograph, this indicates that the animal is shown 3 times larger than its natural size (or whatever number is given).

2 When you study an insect you should use the plan given on page 8.

What are insects?

The insects are **the most important group in the animal world.** They are very numerous; a million species have been identified and described, approximately two-thirds of all animal species.

They are found everywhere: in the grass, in trees, in the soil and in water.

They have many different forms but they are all constructed on the same basic pattern.

The body is made up of three parts: the head, the thorax and the abdomen, protected by an external skeleton that is more or less rigid.

– The head bears
- a pair of antennae
- two large compound eyes (made up of hundreds of tiny facets).

The eyes of insects are made up of tiny facets. Each one is, in essence, a single eye.

Some insects have as many as 25,000 facets. The ant has no more than 50 but the Common Housefly has 4,000, and the dragonfly about 12,000.

You can see the two compound eyes of a hover fly in the photograph.

- special mouthparts are developed which enable them to feed on liquids.

– The thorax carries
- three pairs of jointed legs: this character is typical of all insects.
- two pairs of wings, except in the flies which have only one pair of true wings.

– The abdomen is made up of ring-like segments.

Insects grow by moulting during the first part of their lives; that is to say, they break through and discard their external skeleton, as one might remove a suit of armour, and then construct a larger one. (You can easily find the empty skins of caterpillars and larvae in the wild, discarded by their owners.)

Insects are an extremely ancient group of animals. They were already in existence more than 300 million years ago, as we know from their fossilized remains.

Use this book to discover the variety of insects. The photographs will help you to recognise several well-known examples of insect species before you go out to look for them.

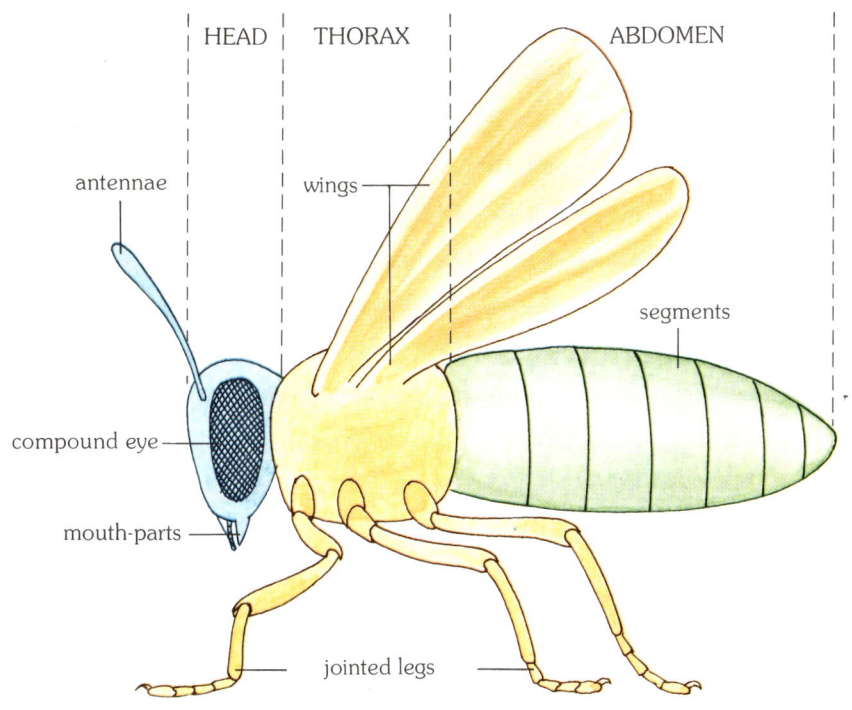

HEAD | THORAX | ABDOMEN

antennae

wings

segments

compound eye

mouth-parts

jointed legs

Diagram of a typical insect, in side view

Each time you look at an insect, identify the various parts indicated in this diagram. You will not always be able to see all of them at once. For example, in this beetle, the front pair of wings are hardened into wing-cases which cover the hind wings and the abdomen completely. But all the other features can be seen. Don't forget to count the legs!

(x 4)

The insect looks like:	TABLE FOR IDENTIFICATION . . .		
	Observe carefully		
	• 2 wings hardened into wing-cases (elytra) • 2 membranous wings protected by the elytra		
	• 2 slightly hardened fore-wings • 2 membranous hind-wings lying beneath		
	• 2 forewings hardened only at the front (hemielytra) • 2 membranous hind-wings lying beneath	Piercing and sucking mouth-parts	
	• All 4 wings membranous	Many finely divided wing-veins	Biting mouth-parts
		Few wing-veins	Piercing and sucking mouth-parts (rostrum)
			Biting and licking mouth-parts
	• All 4 wings covered with scales	Sucking mouth-parts, with the tongue curled in a spiral	
	• Only 2 membranous wings	Licking mouth-parts	
		Piercing mouth-parts	

... OF INSECTS TO STUDY and find its nme		See also pages:	It belongs to the order
Green elytra	**Rose Chafer**	12/13	
Orange elytra with black spots	**Ladybird**	14/15	
Black elytra — short antennae	**Dung Beetle**		COLEOPTERA
Black elytra — long antennae	**Long-horn Beetle**		
Hind-legs adapted for jumping — short antennae	**Grasshopper**	8/9	
Hind-legs adapted for jumping — long antennae	**Cricket**	8/9	
Anterior legs modified as raptorial claws	**Mantis**	10/11	ORTHOPTERA
Anterior legs modified for burrowing	**Mole-cricket**		
Green elytra	**Green Shield-bug**	16/17	
Elytra marked with various colours . .	**Garden bug**	16/17	
Elytra striped with red and black	*Graphosoma* **bug**	16/17	HEMIPTERA– HETEROPTERA
Elytra grey-fawn. Found in ponds . . .	**Backswimmer water bug**	20/21	
Elytra red, flecked with black, no membranous wings visible	**Firebug**	16/17	
	Dragonfly	22/23	ODONATA
	Cicada	18/19	HEMIPTERA– HOMOPTERA
Body furry and thickset — small	**Honey Bee** (worker)		
Body furry and thickset — large	**Honey bee** (drone)		
Body less furry and slimmer — small	**Wasp**		HYMENOPTERA
Body less furry and slimmer — large	**Hornet**		
Body shining and hairless, running and usually without wings	**Ant**		
	Butterfly	26/27/30	LEPIDOPTERA
	Fly		DIPTERA
	Mosquito		

Grasshoppers and crickets

Grasshoppers and crickets are closely related insects which look alike and are often confused. The following table will enable you to distinguish between them and to compare their modes of life.

	Grasshopper	Cricket
Features of the body	● Body stout and hard ● Antennae short and directed forwards	● Body slender and soft ● Antennae long and fine, backwards over the body
	● The fore-wings are straight and hard	
Food	● Grasses in dry meadows	● Grasses, seeds, little worms, grasshoppers, butterflies
	● Both have strongly developed, grinding mandibles (2)	
	● Vegetarian	● Omnivorous
Movement	● Jumping using the long hind legs	
	● Flying using the hind wings (often brightly coloured in some species)	● Flying using the hind wings
	● Active by day	● Active at night
Reproduction	● Male is smaller than the female ● Often found mating. The female carries the male on her back (3)	● Female has a long spine-like tail called the ovipositor (4)
	● Female lays many egg in batches in damp soil	● Female lays eggs singly in in damp soil
	● The young nymphs (2) are identical to their parents but have very short wings, which lengthen at each moult.	
They are eaten by these predators	Praying mantis, snakes, lizards, frogs, toads	

1 In each photograph, which are grasshoppers and which crickets?
2 What are their similarities?
3 Why are grasshoppers and crickets classified as insects?
(see page 4 and page 29)

1

2
(x 6)

3
(x 2)

4
(x 1)

5

The praying mantis

Where can it be found?

The praying mantis is rare but very interesting. It is mainly found in hot countries or in very sunny places in Europe. In September and October it can be seen perched on a twig or grass-stem. The mantis ambushes her prey (grasshoppers, crickets, butterflies, etc.) as it passes her lair. Her attitude (praying) is very characteristic: body held half erect, front claws folded against the thorax, almost in an attitude of prayer. Nevertheless, her attack is made with lightning speed and her cruel claws never release the prey (1).

Life history and development

The egg-cases of the mantis can be found in autumn, glued onto flat stones and twigs. The young mantises hatch in early May – between 50 and 200 from each egg-case (3).

When they leave the egg-case, they vibrate their antennae and their six legs rapidly, and begin to run about quickly, showing exactly the attacking attitude and behaviour of the adult. They are, however, wingless and colourless. After several hours the pigmentation appears and their bodies turn grey.

During its larval life the young mantis moults five times. Its wings will not develop until it becomes an adult, male or female, by August.

Mating takes place at the end of the summer (4). The female lays her eggs in the egg-cases immediately afterwards (2).

The mantis is a very ferocious carnivore, attacking grasshoppers, crickets, and butterflies; it even devours other mantids. However, it is itself the prey of lizards, toads, slow-worms and insectivorous birds.

4 Describe the stages in the life history of the mantis.
5 Construct a food-chain which includes the praying mantis.
6 Why do you think the praying mantis is an insect?

See pages 4 and 29.

1
(x 2)

2

3
(x 1)

4

The ladybird

1
(x 7)

2
(x 5)

This well-known little beetle with orange-red elytra and black spots is very useful in the garden as it is a voracious eater of aphids.

Its life history is easy to observe. In about one month you will be able to see all the stages of its development.

Life history

1. In the Spring or autumn you should begin to collect aphids which you must keep in the following way: Place some potatoes on the surface of some damp soil, making sure that it does not dry out. Introduce into the soil a root of a plant which has been attacked by aphids. The aphids will develop rapidly on the potatoes and become very abundant. They will serve as food for the ladybirds.

2. Now introduce some newly-captured ladybirds. Mating will soon take place. The females lay their eggs about a week later and deposit between 10 and 90 eggs at a time on the surface of the potatoes.

After 3 to 6 days the little larvae will emerge and as they develop you must take care to keep them well fed as they are very voracious.

The **larval life** lasts from 15 to 18 days, during which the larvae grow bigger and moult three times. Then they find shelter under stones or moss and are there transformed into the pupal stage. (Remember to put some moss on the bottom of the rearing cage.) Between 3 and 12 days later, the adult beetles emerge. You can then set them free. The ladybirds live from one to 15 months. They hibernate during the winter, hidden among curled-up leaves or in cracks in the bark of trees; otherwise, they are eaten by insectivorous birds.

1 Ladybird eating aphids **2** Taking flight – note the membranous hind-wings being unfolded **3** Resting **4** Male and female mating **5** Eggs deposited on potatoes **6** A larva **7** An adult beetle, newly emerged from the pupal case

7 Draw a ladybird in outline. Then draw the black spots on the outline.

8 List the different stages in the life-cycle of a ladybird.

9 What are the characters which enable you to say that a ladybird is an insect?

10 What other insects do you know which have two wings hardened into wing-cases, and two wings membranous, like those of the ladybird? (See pages 4 and 29).

The Rose Chafer

Like a jewel in the centre of a flower, the Rose Chafer beetle is half buried in a mass of petals. If you disturb it, it will fly away heavily and noisily. Notice that it is an insect which flies with the elytra closed over the abdomen. There is an opening on each side which allows the membranous hind-wings to be unfolded for flight.

(x 4)

The **adult** lives for about one year. It can hibernate through the winter and in the following Spring it mates, lays its eggs and dies.

The adult Rose Chafer beetle **feeds** on flower petals and stamens (usually those of roses, lilac and elderberry) or ripe fruit, using its strong mandibles.

It has **predators,** of course: birds and insectivorous mammals eat the adult beetle, and centipedes, toads, mole-crickets and moles attack the larvae in the soil.

It is difficult to believe that such a magnificent adult insect should develop from a fat white underground larva – but it is so.

The adult chafers mate during June and the females bury their eggs deep in the soil. The egg hatches after about 12 days and gives rise to a voracious little white larva (1) which **feeds** on decaying vegetable matter.

1
(x 2)

2
(x 1,5)

3
(x 1,5)

4
(x 1,5)

It always lies on its back and remains for two years as a larva in the soil, during which time it grows very large.

When it turns into a pupa it does so inside a rigid cocoon which it makes from plant debris, soil and mud. Look at the photograph (2) which shows the cocoon opened to reveal the pupa inside. At the beginning of August the newly adult Rose Chafer beetle breaks out of the cocoon and leaves the soil (3 and 4) for vegetation, where it develops its brilliant green colour.

11   Compare the life of the adult chafer with that of its larva, and complete a table, for each, showing habitat, movement, food, growth, reproduction, length of life.

12   What kind of environmental conditions stimulate the developing larva of the chafer to leave the soil and later to return to it?

13   Look at the photographs and read the text. What are the features of the Rose Chafer which identify it as an insect?

(See pages 4 and 29.)

The firebug and other plant bugs

(x 3,3)

In the Spring, at the base of trees (limes, elms and poplars) you may find colonies of "soldier bugs" or "firebugs" which congregate together in warm sunny places. They have longish oval bodies, bright red in colour with black markings, and are about a centimetre ($\frac{1}{2}$ in) long. These bugs are flightless, for their hind-wings are reduced in size and have no function.

They are not only vegetable feeders (eating leaves and wild fruit) but will also **feed** on other insects and on dead animals, using a sharp pointed rostrum to pierce their prey. The rostrum normally lies folded backwards under the thorax when not in use.

These bugs **mate** tail-to-tail, facing away from each other (4). The female lays her eggs in the humus layer of the soil. The young nymphs which emerge resemble the adults exactly, except that they have very small wing-cases (hemielytra).

The **predators** of these bugs are insectivorous birds and small mammals such as shrews, moles and hedgehogs.

You can rear these bugs very easily in a "terrarium", a cage containing dead leaves, moss and some pieces of bark to provide shelter. Some of them can only be found in specific limited areas. Nevertheless, it is interesting to know about them – and to look for them if you visit their habitats during your holidays.

1
(x 6)

2
(x 2)

3
(x 1)

4
(x 2)

5
(x 6)

6
(x 3,5)

1 The Pentatomid bug sucks plant sap with the aid of its piercing and sucking mouth-parts (rostrum)   **2** Two pairs of wings are unfolded. Note that the fore-wings are hardened at the base and membranous at the tip. These are called hemielytra and are the reason for calling these bugs Hemiptera, literally "half-wings"   **3** An adult Shield bug with a mass of young nymphs   **4** *Graphosoma*, the Striped Shield bug. The two on the left of the picture are mating   **5** A nymph of the Green Shield bug with very short wing-cases revealing the pattern on the abdomen   **6** A colourful Shield bug

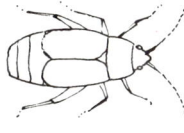

14   Draw a Shield bug in the act of feeding.
15   Colour the drawing of the bug correctly.
16   Why do you think the Shield bug is an insect?
Look at the photographs carefully.
(See pages 4 and 20.)

1 (x 2)

The cicada

This strident "singer" is a native of countries with sunny climates, especially in the Mediterranean area. It is very difficult to see, as it sits motionless in the branches of trees, since its body is almost exactly the colour of bark and its wings are almost transparent.

Like all bugs, the cicada has piercing and sucking mouth-parts and it feeds, using its rostrum, on the sap of trees. The rostrum can be clearly seen in the photograph (1).

Only the male cicada sings (it is called stridulation) using a drum-like membrane on the undersurface of its body (**M** in photograph 2) which is vibrated by the rapid contraction of a muscle in the abdomen. At the least disturbance, the cicada will fly away rapidly with a clattering noise (3).

Cicadas mate in July and August. The females lay their eggs in cracks in the bark of trees or on dry plant stalks. The adults then die at the end of the summer.

When the nymphs hatch from the eggs they fall to the ground and burrow into the soil with their specially modified front legs (4). They feed on tree roots for four years during which time they grow and moult several times.

After four years underground, the nymph leaves the soil in June or July depending on the year, climbs onto a grass stalk (5), then moults for the last time and becomes a fully adult insect (6).

2
(x 1,5)

3
(x 0,75)

4
(x 1)

5
(x 3)

6

17 Compare the life of the adult cicada with that of the nymph. Complete a table for each, showing habitat, movement, food, growth, reproduction, length of life.
18 What are the different stages in the life-cycle of the cicada?
19 Why do you think the cicada is an insect?
(See pages 4 and 30.)

The waterboatman

When approaching a marsh or pond you will often find some water insects lying upside-down and obliquely just below the surface with their abdomen just breaking the surface of the water. These are waterboatmen, known as "Backswimmers". Their Latin name – Notonecta – means "swimming on the back".

If you try to keep one in an aquarium, put a gauze cover on the aquarium because these insects fly actively at night and can easily escape.

If you disturb a Backswimmer, it will swim rapidly away with a few quick strokes of its large and powerful hind-legs. These are fringed with stiff hairs and act just like a pair of oars in a rowing-boat (3 and 4). This water-bug can dive and hold onto the stem of a water-plant. During this period, it consumes the bubble of air which it has carried down attached to little bristles on the abdomen. When it returns to the surface, the tip of the abdomen is protruded to renew the supply of air (1).

Feeding

Waterboatmen feed on tadpoles, eel larvae and all sorts of aquatic insect larvae, as well as those land insects which happen to fall onto the water surface. In attacking its prey the waterboatman first injects a poisonous saliva which kills the prey and then uses the rostrum to suck out its body contents (2).

Do not hold a Backswimmer in your bare hand – it can pierce the skin and give you a painfull "bite". However, the effect soon wears off.

The Backswimmers, like all the waterboatmen, are aquatic bugs.

Mating

Depending on the region in which they live, the waterboatmen mate between October and March. The females lay their eggs in slits which they make in the stems of water-plants. The nymphs closely resemble the adults, except that they are smaller and do not have fully developed wings. They moult several times before reaching full size and developing their wings as adults.

Predators

The Backswimmer, itself a ferocious carnivore, is attacked and eaten by insectivorous birds and also by frogs.

20 Compare the waterboatman with the Shield bugs on pages 16 and 17. What do they have in common.
21 What does the waterboatman have that enables it to swim on its back?
22 Why can the waterboatman be regarded as an insect?
(See pages 4 and 30.)

1
(x 2)

2
(x 6)

Hanging from the water surface, the Backswimmer takes in air while feeding on a fly (**1**). Notice the rostrum folded under the head (**2**).

3
(x 2)

4
(x 2)

Watch the swimming of a waterboatman, noting the three pairs of legs and decide which are used for swimming forwards.

5
(x 2)

6
(x 1,5)

This aquatic insect can leave the water, dry itself (**5**), open its wings (**6**) and fly away.

The dragonfly

Close to any piece of water (river, pond or lake) you will find dragonflies in flight. Watch them carefully. One will rest on a water-plant for several seconds, but it will not move because it can only crawl with difficulty. Then, suddenly, it flies up, lightly and rapidly, sometimes very fast. It can also hover in the air like a helicopter.

It **feeds** on living prey, such as flies, mosquitoes and mayflies, all of which it can easily catch in flight. The handsome dragonfly is a **carnivore**.

Its own **predators** are frogs, toads and birds.

The dragonfly nymph

The eggs hatch soon after being laid and the dragonfly nymphs develop slowly under water for several years (2 to 5) according to the species, and moult a dozen times.

The dragonfly nymph breathes through leaf-like gills at the extreme end of the abdomen. It crawls along the bottom of ponds in search of prey but when disturbed it shoots rapidly forward by spurting a jet of water out of its tail – like a jet-propelled escape mechanism.

This voracious nymph hunts by ambushing its prey. It attacks living prey – tadpoles, young fish and other insects – which it catches with its mask, a kind of jointed lower lip armed with sharp claws which is folded under the head (2). When a suitable prey animal passes its lair, the mask is shot forward, the claws grasping the animal and drawing it back to the mouth which is supplied with strong mandibles (3).

Luckily for the rest of the pondlife, the dragonfly nymph is itself the victim of carnivorous fish.

When it is fully grown, the nymph transforms into the adult dragonfly. Photographs 4 to 7 show the emergence of the adult from a nymph which has crawled out of the water onto a plant stem. The beautiful coloration of the adult dragonfly develops slowly as it expands and dries its wings.

23 Compare the nymph and the adult dragonfly, Complete a table for each, showing habitat, movement, feeding, growth, reproduction, length of life.

24 Why is the dragonfly an insect?

(See pages 4 and 31.)

1
(x 1,5)

2
(x 1,5)

3
(x 4)

In photographs 2 and 3, note the mask (m), armed with hook-like claws (c), which are used to catch a tadpole before it is devoured.

4   **5**   **6**   **7**

By reference to photograph 1 and the drawings on page 31, you can make a model dragonfly, using polystyrene for the body, transparent paper or plastic for the wings, some electrical wire for the legs and the antennae, and sequins for the eyes. The diagram on page 4 will help you.

The mating of dragonflies

The coupling of dragonflies is quite spectacular and it is preceded by a mating flight. After mating, the female lays several thousand tiny eggs which she inserts into the stems of water-plants, or else drops freely into the water. The adults live only for a few months.

2 The male seizes the female by the head

1 The male transfers his sperm to a special pouch in the first segment of the abdomen

3 The female places her genital aperture onto the male's abdomen to receive the sperm

4 The female lays her eggs "under the supervision of the male"

P. MORIN

1 Look! a male pursuing a female

2 He flies past her and then releases a chemical called a pheromone from his abdomen. This attracts her to him

3 So that's how it's done. She is seduced by his perfume!

4 He flutters down onto the female several times and caresses her with his antennae

6 Missed! The male has carried the female away for the nuptial flight

5 Let's try to catch them while they are mating

P. NORIN

The Cabbage White butterfly

1
(x 1)

2
(x 1)

The Cabbage White is a very common butterfly. It is greenish-white with blackish markings on the wings. The **male** (**1**) and the **female** (**2**) have different markings

3

4
(x 3)

You will be able to catch these butterflies in the garden during April. After mating (**3**), the female lays 100 to 200 eggs under cabbage or nasturtium leaves (**4**)

5
(x 10)

6
(x 1)

The caterpillars hatch about a week after the eggs are laid (**5**) and begin to devour the leaves of the **host plant**. The caterpillars grow rapidly over a period of 15 to 25 days (**6**). They moult four or five times before becoming fully grown

7
(x 1)

8

9
(x 2)

When they are fully grown, the caterpillars stop moving about and attach the abdomen by a little silk pad to a firm support. Each caterpillar then spins a fine silk loop around the middle of the body and attaches it to the supporting stem, leaf or piece of wood. It then moults a last time and turns into a **chrysalis** (**7**). Although normally motionless, the chrysalis is sensitive and will wriggle in its silken loop if you disturb it. It remains like this for 8 to 10 days. Then major changes begin to take place inside the chrysalis.

All the organs of the caterpillar are transformed to give rise to those of the adult insect, the butterfly (**9**). When this is completed, the skin of the chrysalis splits open (in the middle of the thorax and the head) and the butterfly slowly pulls itself out of the discarded skin. It unfolds its soft and crumpled wings which then dry out and harden and enable it to fly away in search of its food, the nectar from flowers (**10**).

10

Parasitism

You will be surprised sometimes to find that your caterpillar which seemed so healthy is parasitised by many tiny white larvae which crawl out of its body and spin tiny cocoons of yellow silk, often on the caterpillar itself (**11**). Then, after several days, you will find that they have produced a number of tiny parasitic wasps, belonging to the Hymenoptera. These are *Apanteles*, a common parasite of the Cabbage White cater-

11

pillar. The female wasp lays her eggs directly into the body of the caterpillar.

25 Try to construct a diagram showing the life-cycle of the butterfly.
26 Compare the caterpillar with the adult.
27 Say why butterflies can be classified as insects. (See pages 4 and 31.)

The caterpillar (**1**), the chrysalis (**2**) and the head (**3**) of a Swallowtail butterfly x7

The Swallowtail butterfly (**4**)

The caterpillar (**5**) and the adult Garden Tiger moth (**6**)

Answers to questions

---------------- **Grasshoppers and crickets** ----------------

1. Photographs 1, 2 and 3: grasshoppers. Photographs 4 and 5: crickets.
2. They have the same features: forewings straight and hard
with biting, crushing mandibles.
They both jump and can fly.
The young nymphs are identical to their parents.

---------------- **Praying mantis** ----------------

4. Life history

Egg laid in	→	Hatching in	→	5 moults	→	Adults in	⟨ males or females ⟩	→	Mating	→	eggs
autumn		May		during the summer		August					in autumn

5. Food chain (an example)

Grasshopper — is eaten by → Praying mantis — is eaten by → Lizard

---------------- **Ladybird beetle** ----------------

7.

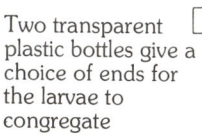

Adult   Larva

8. Life history

Adults ⟨ males or females ⟩ Mating — 1 week → Eggs — 3 to 6 days → Larva — 3 moults / 15 to 18 days → Pupa — 3 to 12 days → ⟨ males or females ⟩ Adults

10. Rose Chafer, dung beetle, long-horn beetle

---------------- **Rose Chafer** ----------------

Adult   Larva (white grub)

11.

	Habitat	Food	Movement	Growth	Reproduction	Length of life
Adult	Aerial	Flowers/fruit	Flight/walking	✕	Yes	1 year
Larva	Underground	Vegetable debris	Moves on its back	Yes	✕	2 years

12. The larvae leaving the soil seek daylight and those returning seek darkness.

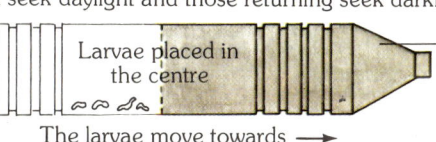

Black paper covering half the apparatus

Larvae placed in the centre

Two transparent plastic bottles give a choice of ends for the larvae to congregate

The larvae move towards → the darkened area

14.    **15.**

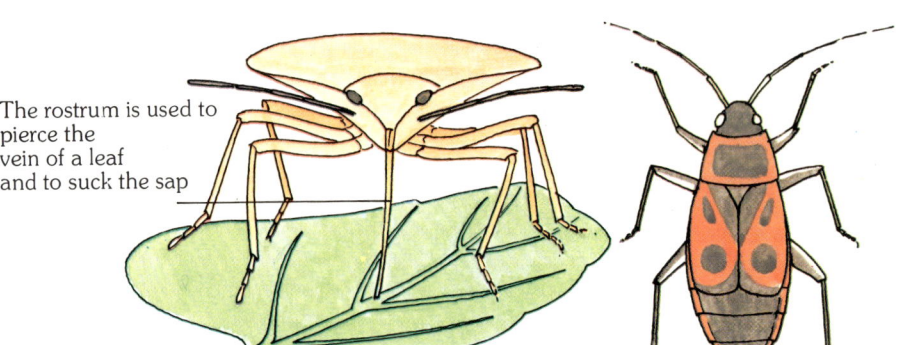

The rostrum is used to pierce the vein of a leaf and to suck the sap

Cicada

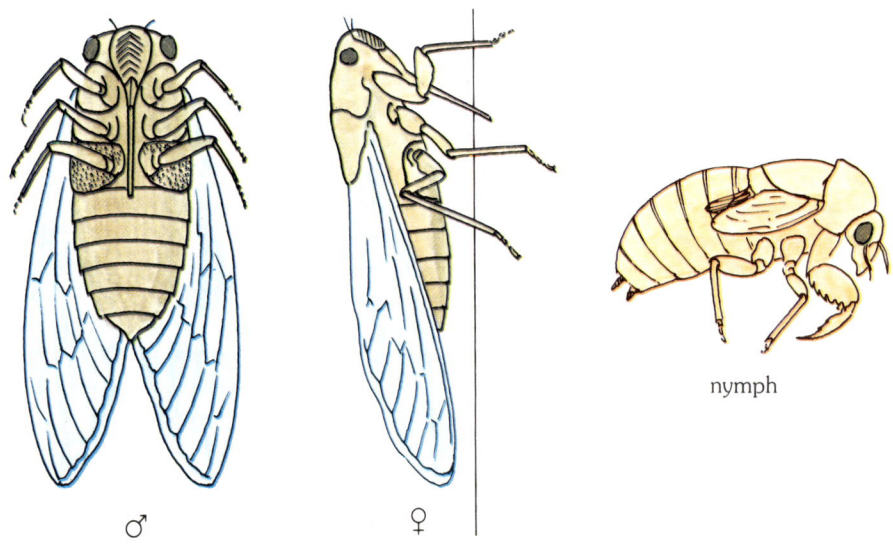

nymph

♂   ♀

17.	Habitat	Food	Movement	Growth	Reproduction	Length of life
Adult	aerial	sap	flying		Yes	2 months
Nymph	underground	roots	digging	Yes		4 years

18. The life history of the cicada

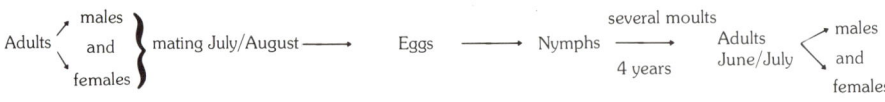

Adults ↗ males
        and } mating July/August ⟶ Eggs ⟶ Nymphs ⟶ several moults / 4 years ⟶ Adults June/July ↗ males
        ↘ females   and
                                                                                                     ↘ females

Waterboatmen

20. – The fore-wings are half-hardened and cover the membranous hind-wings which are used for flying.
– A rostrum, which is used to pierce the prey.
21. Its back is streamlined like the hull of a boat and its long hind-legs propel it, functioning like a pair of oars.

23.	Habitat	Food	Movement	Growth	Reproduction	Length of life
Adult	aerial	insects	flying		Yes	several months
Nymph	aquatic	tadpoles, fish and other larvae	crawling and swimming	Yes		2 to 5 years

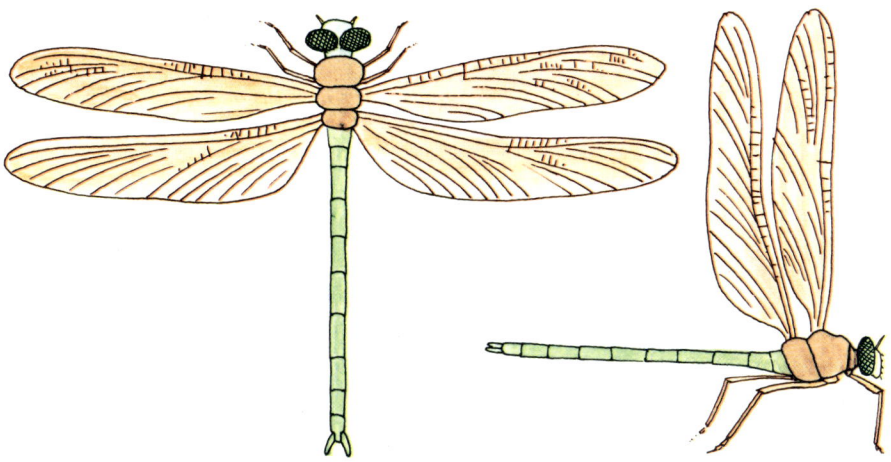

Copy these drawings
Label the different parts of the dragonfly with reference to the diagram on page 5.

Cabbage White butterfly

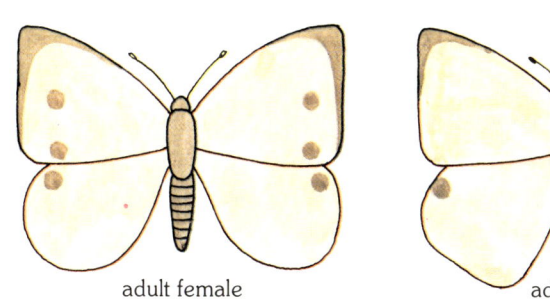

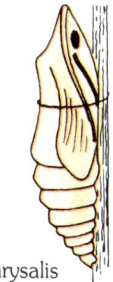

adult female   adult male   chrysalis

25. Life history of the butterfly

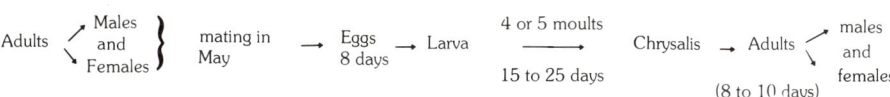

Adults { Males and Females } mating in May → Eggs 8 days → Larva — 4 or 5 moults — 15 to 25 days → Chrysalis → Adults { males and females (8 to 10 days)

26.	Habitat	Food	Movement	Growth	Reproduction	Length of life
Butter-fly	aerial	nectar of flowers	flying		Yes	2 to 3 weeks
Cater-pillar	crawling on plants	leaves	crawling	Yes		15 to 25 days

31

First published in the English language 1983
© Burke Publishing Company Limited 1983
Translated and adapted from *Peuple des insectes: Collection Bornancin-Mérigot*
© Editions Fernand Nathan 1981

Acknowledgements
The publishers are grateful to Dr. R. C. Fisher for preparing the text of this edition, and to the following for permission to reproduce copyright illustrations:
    Bornancin, Chaumeton-Lanceau, Coleman, Jacana, Pitch, Six, Tarlier. *Cover:* Jacana.
The drawings are by Patrick Morin.

CIP data
The world of insects. – (Wake up to the world of science)
    1. Insects
    I. Bornancin, B.   II. Mérigot, M.   II. Le peuple des insectes. *English*
    IV. Series
    595.7   QK467.2
    ISBN 0 222 00871 7
    ISBN 0 222 00872 5 Pbk.

Burke Publishing Company Limited
Pegasus House, 116-120 Golden Lane, London EC1Y 0TL, England.
Burke Publishing (Canada) Limited
Toronto, Ontario, Canada.
Burke Publishing Company Inc.
540 Barnum Avenue, Bridgeport, Connecticut 06608, U.S.A.
Filmset in "Monophoto" Souvenir by Green Gates Studios, Hull, England.
Printed in the Netherlands by Deltaprint Holland.